BISI & TOYIN TOFADE

practical outlines for success in marriage

REVIVE · RENEW · REKINDLE

Practical Outlines for Success in Marriage
Drs. Bisi & Toyin Tofade

All rights reserved. No portion of this book may be reproduced in any form without the written permission of the authors.

Printed in the United States of America

Copyright © by Drs. Bisi & Toyin Tofade

Unless otherwise indicated, Scriptures are taken from the King James Version of the Bible.

ISBN 978-1-60924-052-3

Library of Congress Control Number: 2015934920

For More information, contact the authors at:
Jubilee Christian Church Int'l
4809 Prospectus Dr.
Durham, NC 27713
practicaloutlines@gmail.com
Website: www.delightfulbooks.net

Triumph Publishing
P. O. Box 690158
Bronx, New York 10469
718-652-7157
www.triumphpublishing.net

Table of Contents

Healthy Marriages — 11
What Constitutes a Healthy Relationship? — 11
Spelling a Healthy Marriage — 15
3 Simple Things To Remember and Do Daily — 20
Recipe For a Healthy Marriage — 20
Sex in Marriage — 25
Tips To Stimulate Romance in Your Spouse — 27
Renewal of Vows — 28

The Little Foxes That Ruin Marriages — 33
What Are These Little Foxes? — 33
It's all about Communication — 35
What Not to Say to Your wife — 39
What Not to Say to Your husband — 39
Simple Things to Spoil Your Mate and Spice Up Your Marriage — 40

Better or Bitter Marriage — 47
Stages of Marriage — 47
7 Commandments of Marriage — 48
Bad Habits That Could Ruin Your Marriage! — 49
10 Steps to A Better Marriage — 55

Managing Conflict And Crisis In Marriage — 65
Is Your Marriage in Crisis? — 65
3 Forces that Fight Against our Homes: The Warning signs — 66

Major Causes of Marital Conflict	67
The Place of Money	68
The Issue of The In-Laws	81

Conflict Styles — 89

Keys to Resolving Marital Conflict	91
What to do to Fix a Marriage in Crisis	92
Abuse in Marriage	99
Marriage and Infidelity	105

Marriage And Divorce — 117

What Is Divorce?	118
Phases of Divorce	120
The Implications or Cost of Advice	120

Single Parents — 125

Parenting Alone	125
Dealing With Your Ex	127
Coping With Loneliness	129

Bibliography	135

Endorsement

From the beginning of creation marriage was designed to be a blessing and not a curse.

Everything that God created was said to be good. But after God created man in Genesis 2:18 *'And the LORD God said, it is not good that the man should be alone; I will make him an help meet for him'*

The goal of God in making a woman for the man in marriage is to be a help meet, that is a suitable helper, not a liability, nor a burden, not a curse or additional problems of life.

Marriage is supposed to be a blessing and not a medium of frustration. Anywhere you see anything in marriage that cannot be described as good, something is wrong.

In this book, Drs. Bisi and Toyin Tofade indicated some very important truths that will make any marriage to reflect God's dream for marriage. It is my belief that any home passing through some challenges right now will find useful information that will bring about a desired change for better in the marriage. I therefore recommend this book for those planning to get married and those already married.

Rev (Dr.) Kunle Adesina.
General overseer
Jubilee Christian Church Int'l

Introduction

This book was written for the novices, the beginners and the matured in marriage. It is for those who wonder what marriage is all about, for those who are rushing to get in and for those who are tired and rushing to get out of it.

Within this book are practical and easy to follow steps presented in outline format that every couple can use to find out what is wrong with their relationship and what they can do to fix the problems.

Success in marriage is more than finding the right person, it is a matter of being the right person...

Reflection

Marriage Is An Investment
That Pays Dividends, If You Pay
The Premiums.

Healthy Marriages

Marriage is supposed to be a peaceful environment in which two consenting and loving adults acknowledge their individual imperfections and adapt to one another in Holy Matrimony. Marriage should be a place of mutual submission, love and willingness to adapt to one another.

> *Ephesians 5:33 (AMP)*
>
> *However, let each man of you [without exception] love his wife as [being in a sense] his very own self; and let the wife see that she respects and reverences her husband [that she notices him, regards him, honors him, prefers him, venerates, and esteems him; and that she defers to him, praises him, and loves and admires him exceedingly].*

Marriage is supposed to make you into a better person, not a bitter one. Many people today are married but not merry; they are married and regretful. Their lives are filled with a lot of anger and pain, tons of buried bitterness and permeated by an unforgiving spirit.

Many are having stress in their relationships. For countless people, it is a constant fight all day, including weeks of holding on to grudges, months of keeping malice and years of harboring bitterness. Constant conflicts and frictions, truck and lorry loads of unhappiness burden them. Is this what marriage is meant to be?

Marriage is meant to complement you, not complicate your life. It is meant to add and complete you, not subtract and reduce you. Marriages can be made in heaven, but man is responsible for the maintenance work on earth.

What constitutes a healthy relationship?

A healthy relationship is one in which the husband loves and protects his wife unconditionally and unreservedly. He saves her from the attacks of external parties, in-laws, individuals, the devil and sometimes herself! A healthy relationship is on in which a wife adapts, submits and defers to the man as stated in Ephesians 5:33. Submission is when you choose to stoop to conquer, and is by no means a suggestion that you are stupid, or less intelligent. It is an understanding of spiritual authority in marriage.

In healthy marriage, you find the following:

1. **Joy peace and harmony**
   - Environment of trust collaboration, cooperation, peace, humility, gratitude and respect for one another.
   - Where peace is missing, progress is impossible.
   - Anything or anyone that steals your peace is not good for you, find a resolution quickly.

   Proverbs 17:1 (KJV)

   Better is a dry morsel, and quietness therewith, than a house full of sacrifices with strife.

2. **No abuse, misuse and domination**

   Some marriages border on abuse. They are more like the relationship between a master and servant instead of a healthy relationship. Such relationships are characterized by...
   - Verbal abuse, cursing, manipulative behavior, ultimatums, dictatorships and so on.

   Proverbs 21:9 (KJV)

   It is better to dwell in a corner of the housetop, than with a brawling woman in a wide house.

What is the value of a big "house" that is not a "home"?

Proverbs 21:9 (Msg)

Better to live alone in a tumbledown shack than share a mansion with a nagging (crabby) spouse.

- Physical Abuse
- Mental/emotional abuse

A man who curses and abuses his wife will raise sons who are prone to do the same. He will also raise daughters who will expect same kind of treatment from their husbands.

Women who ridicule and belittle their husbands will raise daughters who have no respect for men. They will also raise sons who lack the power to lead.

3. Compliments your life not complicate it.

You become a better person when some things are added to your life. There are folks whose lives became complicated since the day they got married. Peace left their lives. That is not the plan of God.

The day Delilah came into Samson's life, his life took a downward turn.

Many people are not in a healthy relationship. The relationship they have with their spouses border on abuse, misuse and being constantly taken advantage of. They are not happy!

Healthy kids grow and thrive effortlessly. All you need to do to have healthy children is to feed them. In certain cultures, parents regularly administer medicine to de-worm young children. No matter what you eat or where you live, if you have an infestation of worms, it will show on you. You will look malnourished!

Many marriages have worms! Some were infected with worms after few months of marriage. These worms are crawling all over their marriages and sucking out the joyful juice in their homes. If you endure your marriage instead of enjoying it you may have a malnourished marriage.

Worm of selfishness

In unhealthy marriages selfishness reigns, and it is often responsible for destroying many unions. The definition of marriage has quickly become the association of two unhappy people thinking that they can get their happiness at the expense of their spouse.

- To be happy, think of what you can give, not what you want or can take. In other words, instead of looking for the right person, be the right person.

- If you want to be happy, endeavor to make your mate happy. Learn to spell Joy correctly…Jesus first, Yourself last and Others in between!

Worm of bitterness, anger and un-forgiveness

- Piles of unforgiven hurts and offences. There is no doubt that we will offend one another, so we must use forgiveness generously. If you harbor resentment, it will choke you and clog your heart.

Worm of poor communication.

- People in unhealthy relationships don't know how to talk to each other. They yell, shout and raise their voices and fists, yet they want to call that communication! If your spouse is nagging, this is evidence that you are a poor listener.

Effective communication is a must in order to keep your honeymoon flowing.

- Never keep or hide your feelings from your mate.
- Express yourself in love and courtesy.
- Listen to your spouse's feelings. Don't interrupt.
- Remember that you cannot always be right.

A woman wakes up one night to find that her husband of twenty years is not in bed. This is unusual, so she gets up to find him. She looks in the bathroom, and in the kitchen, and is becoming alarmed when she hears terrible sobbing and moaning coming from the basement. She goes to the basement, and asks him why he's crying. He replies, "Do you remember when your daddy caught us having sex in the back of my car when you were sixteen?" She says, "Yes, how can I forget that?" He says, "Do you remember what he told me that night?" She says, "Sure I do. He told you that if you didn't marry me you'd spend the next twenty years of your life in prison. So why are you crying?"

He said, "Well, it just occurred to me that I'd be getting out this week."

—Jack Martin, Lubbock, TX

Spelling A Healthy Marriage
To stay healthy....spell H-E-A-L-T-H-Y

Honesty...

- Honesty is the best policy. Don't practice lies in your marriage.
- Never lie to your spouse. Let your yes be yes!
- No secrets, no hidden agenda, embrace openness.
- No secret password or private enterprise.
- Lie not to one another....Col. 3:9
- Be transparent. The man and the woman were both naked... Gen 2:25

Empathy...

- Express kindness, affection and compassion to one another and put value on your spouse.
- In an unhealthy marriage, couples take one another for granted. This can be compared to when you buy a new car, you spend time with it and treat it with care, but when it becomes old and worn...you slam the door, you change the grade of gas you feed it.
- What you "feed" into your spouse is what you get out of them. Call her stupid, and you get stupid behavior. Treat her like queen; you will get a royal product from her.
- You ignore one another and treat each other like trash. No wonder the whole house stinks!

Appreciate...

- Be grateful for little things, don't take one another for granted. Don't say "it is your duty" to do x, y and z, be thankful. Thank you is a magic word, use it generously and regularly.
- Ingratitude is a bad attitude, avoid it like the plague.

- Thank your partner for your clean clothes, the beautiful meals, the dust free house, the clean sheets and the free sex – she will love you for it. Thank him for being a provider, a great dad, a lover and protector. He will feel on top of the world.
- If she makes the money in the house, make sure she is appreciated for it.
- If you appreciate your spouse, the value of your marriage will not depreciate.
- Continually say positive things to your spouse.
- Don't compare your spouse with others.

Ephesians 4:29

Don't use foul or abusive language. Let everything you say be good and helpful, so that your words will be an encouragement to those who hear them.

Love....

Love Acronym

Listens actively

Overlooks faults

Values and validates voluminously

Encourages endlessly

- Love is the platform for any meaningful relationship.
- When love is missing, you only endure the union, you don't enjoy it.
- Kindle the flame: romance, touch, time, tenderness.

1 Corinthians 13:4-8 (AMP)

4 Love endures long and is patient and kind; love never is envious nor boils over with jealousy, is not boastful or vainglorious, does not display itself haughtily.

5 It is not conceited (arrogant and inflated with pride); it is not rude (unmannerly) and does not act unbecomingly. Love (God's love in us) does not insist on its own rights or its own way, for it is not self-seeking; it is not touchy or fretful or resentful; it takes no account of the evil done to it [it pays no attention to a suffered wrong].

6 It does not rejoice at injustice and unrighteousness, but rejoices when right and truth prevail.

7 Love bears up under anything and everything that comes, is ever ready to believe the best of every person, its hopes are fadeless under all circumstances, and it endures everything [without weakening].

8 Love never fails [never fades out or becomes obsolete or comes to an end]. As for prophecy (the gift of interpreting the divine will and purpose), it will be fulfilled and pass away; as for tongues, they will be destroyed and cease; as for knowledge, it will pass away [it will lose its value and be superseded by truth].

Trust...

- If trust is broken, the heart is broken and the foundation is shaken.

- Where there is mistrust, you constantly think that your spouse is going to hurt you. You are dishonest with each other.

- You don't believe their words; you feel that they are lying to you.

- They have lost your confidence, you persuade yourself now and then to trust them.

- Seemingly small things erode your relationship, like trickling water that wears away at a rock over time.

Proverbs 31:11 (AMP)

The heart of her husband trusts in her confidently and relies on and believes in her securely, so that he has no lack of [honest] gain or need of [dishonest] spoil.

Honor...

- Remember the law of respect in marriage, put value on your spouse. No verbal abuse, physical abuse or emotional abuse. Don't drag down one another before kids, friends, etc.

- Respect yourself and your spouse.

- Never shout at your spouse or insult him/her, particularly in front of a stranger. Never express anger in the presence of a third party. Instead, affirm your spouse in front of others

- Admit your mistakes; learn to apologize.

- Respect their space, respect what they want and the way they want it.

- Respect your spouse's views and opinion even if seems absurd to you.

Yes...

Marriage is about compromise, you get some, and you give some.

- For peaceful marriage, there must be agreement, harmony, and unity. Joint decision making, complementing one another

- Love is compromise, not insisting on having your own way.

- It's okay to be right and quiet!

- It's okay to give 100%.

- It's okay to compromise.

- Marriage is when you agree to spend the rest of your life sleeping in a room that's too warm, beside someone who's sleeping in a room that's too cold.

A couple was married for sixty years. When asked the reason for their successful marriage, the wife said, "I fell in love often." She paused, then said, "With the same man."

Magic Words in a Relationship

- Thank You
- I am Sorry
- I was wrong
- I should have handled it differently
- Forgive me
- How can I make this right with you?
- I appreciate you

3 Simple things to remember and do daily

1. **Attention**: True Listening.
2. **Affection**: Deeply Caring.
3. **Appreciation**: Noticing minute details of life and expressing gratitude for them.

Recipe For A Happy Marriage

Take a cup of love, two cups of loyalty, three cups of forgiveness, four quarts of faith, and one barrel of laughter. Take love and loyalty and mix them thoroughly with faith; blend the mixture with tenderness, kindness, and understanding. Add friendship and hope. Sprinkle abundantly with laughter. Bake it with sunshine. Wrap it regularly with lots of hugs. Serve generous helpings daily, and you've got a marvelous recipe for a happy marriage.

— Adapted

...Say YES, YES and YES

Discussion Notes

Is your marriage healthy? If not why?

_____

_____

_____

What are the ingredients missing in your marriage that need immediate attention?

_____

_____

_____

Take Action Together

What practical things are you willing to do to make your marriage healthy?

_____

_____

_____

How can magic words like "thank you" and "I am sorry" etc. help your marriage?

_____

_____

Reflection

"In the word 'wedding,'
the 'We' comes before the I"

Sex in Marriage

Men want sex! Women want intimacy. A lot of tension and discord may occur in your marriage if the issue of sex is mishandled. Women may go a long time without having sex as long as they enjoy intimacy, this however is not true for men who tend to experience intimacy through sex.

3 main reasons for sex:

1. A way to prevent temptation (fornication and adultery) 1 Cor 7:1-2

2. A source of communication and pleasure. Prov. 5:18-19

3. A means of procreation. Gen 4:1

Sex is:

- A marital vow that should be kept.

- A responsibility that should be fulfilled.

- Not a weapon or tool used to punish or manipulate a partner.

The Issues Surrounding Sex

Common excuses and phrases used around sex

Women

- If I allow him to touch me as he wants, I become pregnant repeatedly.
- Sorry, I have headache, upset stomach, back ache etc.
- I usually allow him when I need to get him to buy something for me.
- I know where to punish him.
- I am fasting please!
- "How I got the last baby? That day he asked me to go and retrieve something from under the pillow, before I knew it, he came in, and shut the door. It almost looked like rape!"

Men

- We must have it now even if you are dead tired.
- My wife is not submissive…because I am sex-starved

Here is a list of things that can kill sexual drive

Mood killers:

- Uncaring attitudes in word and action.
- Body odor, bad breath.
- Selfishness.
- Impatience of the man in waiting for the wife to reach climax
- Distractions (TV, kids, shores, cooking, laundry etc.)

- Tiredness.
- Strife, arguments and misunderstanding.
- Illness.
- Bitterness, unresolved conflict, unforgiven actions.

Tips to Stimulate Romance in Your Spouse

1. Give her lots of long hugs just because; hug her in the bathroom, in the bedroom, in the kitchen whether she is angry or she is happy. Hug her a lot!
2. Cuddle for intimacy and not just when you want sex.
3. Say kind things about her and to her.
4. Submit to one another, don't try, expect or insist to always have your way.
5. Listen, listen, and listen to her. Do not interrupt. It is as bad as an interrupted orgasm!
6. State what you liked about what your spouse did during your last sex episode.
7. Keep your bedroom neat and tidy, free of clutter and in a romantic mood.
8. Watch romantic movies together.
9. Don't give excuses such as you have a headache or start other 'important issues' when he is ready
10. When you have "attained orgasm" and she has not, don't say "Oh, I have to make a call quick" Let it wait.

11. Be sensitive to movements that can quench an imminent orgasm for her. Continue to give her pleasure even after you have climaxed. Don't fall asleep!

12. Be patient, ask what her preference is, do not assume.

13. Shower her with praise and positive feedback.

14. Tease her, play with her hair, her fingers or whatever she prefers, play hide and seek.

15. Go out together to eat without the kids.

16. Write her a poem documenting your feelings for her.

17. Have a candlelit dinner.

18. Have a bubble bath together.

19. Give each other 10 minute back rubs/massages.

20. Call her at work, go through much trouble just to say I love you.

21. Write her a love note, text or posting.

Renewal of Vows

Sample of renewal vows you and your spouse may share with each other yearly or as often as you desire.

Today, in the presence of God, I renew my vows to you, pledging my eternal love for you, and eagerly awaiting what life may bring us.

I believe in this marriage more than ever, and I reaffirm my love and commitment to you.

"You are mine, my love, and I am yours, as ordained by God from the beginning of time. God brought us together, kept us together.

You are God's gift to me, my priceless treasure, my blessing for life. May God bless us as we come together to renew our pledge of love to one another.

It is with joy born of experience and trust that I commit myself once again to be your (husband/wife)." In the Name of the Father, the Son and the Holy Ghost.

Father, we present our union, our home to you again,

Shield our homes from winds of adversity, the storm of divorce and the aggression of demons. Pour fresh wine of love, joy and peace into our hearts. Let your peace reign supremely

Preserve our lives that we enjoy one another for a long time. Let your blessings flow into our Union.

Protect our children from evil forces of hell. Provide all that is needed to make our homes joyous and fulfilling.

Discussion Notes

What are the factors that prevent sexual satisfaction in your marriage?

_____

_____

_____

What do you like about your sex life? What could be different?

_____

_____

_____

Take Action Together

How do we create an environment where both our sexual needs are satisfied?

_____

_____

_____

What can we do to make sure both parties attain orgasm on a regular basis?

_____

_____

_____

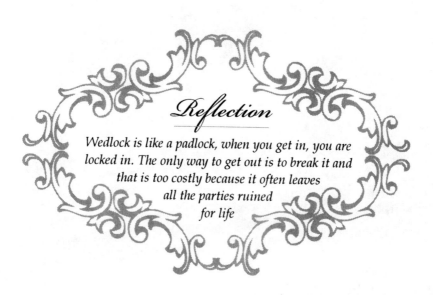

Reflection

Wedlock is like a padlock, when you get in, you are locked in. The only way to get out is to break it and that is too costly because it often leaves all the parties ruined for life

The Little Foxes that Ruin Marriages

The little things that disrupt peace and cause disruption within our marriages

Song of Songs 2:15 (KJV)

Take us the foxes, the little foxes, that spoil the vines: for our vines have tender grapes.

Most often today, it is not the big things that ruin many marriages, it is the small things that over time escalate and become huge and uncontrollable. If we nip a lot of these little things at the bud, our homes will blossom.

What Are These Little Foxes?

1. **Indifference, Ignoring and Neglect (Apathy)**

    Apathy in marriage is a silent killer. It quickly deteriorates the fabric of what makes a healthy relationship. It sends signals of 'not being wanted' or 'needed' by your spouse.

    - Being ignored sends the message that the person doesn't care and it hurts deeply. It could lead to:

        a. Emotional and physical abandonment.
        b. Mental torture.

Signs of Apathy in your Marriage
   i. Sleeping in different bedrooms for no good reason.
   ii. Prolonged lack of intimacy.
   iii. Each mate does his/her own thing without regard for the other.
   iv. Going days, or even weeks without communication.

2. **Taking your partner for granted**
   - Disrespect is associated with taking people for granted.
   - Another symptom of this is a lack of appreciation for your spouse.
   - When a couple takes one another for granted, it depreciates their worth and the value of their marriage.

   What are the symptoms of this in marriage?

3. **Lack Of Appreciation (Ingratitude)**
   - Ingratitude is a bad attitude. Remember your "Please" and "Thank You".
   - Make gratitude your lifestyle, it creates the atmosphere of being relevant and needed.
   - Ingratitude takes people for granted with an underline tone of 'I deserve this'.

4. **Lack Or Loss Of Respect**

   How do you know when your marriage is over? Loss of respect is one of the most obvious and probably the most devastating signs. Little things your spouse does that you used to find endearing start to really annoy you.
   - Respect is a reasonable expectation from your spouse.

- Respect their space, respect what they want and the way they want it.

- Respect your spouse's views and opinion even if you find them absurd.

- Respect means revering and regarding your spouse.

Ephesians 5:33 (AMP)

However, let each man of you [without exception] love his wife as [being in a sense] his very own self; and let the wife see that she respects and reverences her husband [that she notices him, regards him, honors him, prefers him, venerates, and esteems him; and that she defers to him, praises him, and loves and admires him exceedingly].

What makes a man lose respect from his wife?

- Lack of integrity.
- Abusive treatment of wife.
- When he doesn't respect himself.
- Broken promises, unreliable or empty words.

It's all about Communication

5. **Careless Words, Verbal Abuse**
   a. Avoid using threats like:
      i. "I will leave you" or I will divorce you".
      ii. "I will stop cooking" or "no more sex in this house".
      iii. "I will find myself a better spouse elsewhere".

   Threats and the use of ultimatums will only aggravate your spouse and complicate disagreements.

If we guard against these little verbal foxes and keep our vineyards safe and healthy, the fruits of our marriage will be sweet and tender.

b. Watch the tone of your voice.

c. Avoid hurtful words.

Identify words that hurt versus words that heal.

6. **Nagging**

    Case: Ken Mac Dougall bit into the sandwich his wife had packed him for lunch and noticed something odd – a Post-it note tucked between the ham and the cheese. He pulled it out of his mouth, smoothed the crinkles and read what his wife had written: "Be in aisle 10 of Home Depot tonight at 6 p.m., don't be late…this is the tenth time."
    "I thought the note was an ingenious and hysterical way to get his attention," says his wife. "I don't need a reminder in the middle of my sandwich," he says.

    —Wall Street Journal | ELIZABETH BERNSTEIN

    Nagging is found to be one of the topmost marriage killers by experts.

Why Is It So Hard to Stop Nagging?

Nagging kills relationships, because it is an attempt by the spouse to turn the home into a workplace. What person wants to work for a boss and then come home after expecting relaxation only to find yet another boss making demands?

Proverbs 15:1 (KJV)

A soft answer turneth away wrath: but grievous words

Solutions to Nagging

- Stop assuming he/she did not hear you the first time.

- Try a different approach.
- Don't give orders or use a commanding tone.
- Say what you mean, don't go around it.

Who nags more? Men or women?

Often times, men are to blame when women nag. Often, it is because they are not listening when their wives are complaining. Nagging is the result of repeatedly passing out the same information or instructions.

7. **Criticism**

    A negative or critical spirit can easily ruin a marriage and demoralize partners. It is characterized by the following:

    - Fault finding spirit, hunting for the mistakes that your spouse have made.
    - A "gotcha" mindset.
    - Saying "This is your fault". Playing the blame game.
    - "When are you going to get it right?"

We should …

- Avoid the use of "you never…" or "you always…" in your language.

To 'bury' your spouse's Good Idea (negative criticism) say:

- It will never work.
- We've never done it that way before.
- We're doing fine without it.
- We can't afford it.

- We're not ready for it.
- It's not our responsibility. (Bits & Pieces, June 23, 1994)

To criticize constructively in marriage:
- Choose your time and place prudently.
- Start with their strengths and offer commendation.
- Be polite and brief.
- Select your words carefully.
- Focus on issues, not on personality.
- Avoid being emotional.
- End positively.

8. **Anger, Being Unforgiving And Score Keeping**
   - Playing Tit for tat.
   - Insults, yelling, name calling, throwing things, raised voice or hands, banging your fist on the furniture.
   - "I will take vengeance for all the wrong you did to me."
   - Holding on to 20 year old grudges, looking for the right opportunity for payback.

9. **Too Busy, No More Fun Time**

   When couples are too busy, it encroaches on the time they have available for relaxation and fun. Spending time together have positive effect on marital relationships.

In summary, watch your tone in communication
- Don't talk loud, don't yell.

- Don't talk down to your spouse.
- Avoid derogatory and triggering remarks.
- Pay attention to your body language!

<u>What not to say to your wife:</u>

1. "You are becoming too fat these days, what size do you wear again?"
2. "You are just like your mother."
3. "If you don't like it, you can just leave."
4. "Can't you do anything right in this house?"
5. "I don't know why I put up with somebody like you. You are my mistake."
6. "You are boring!"
7. "You should be more like…"
8. "I don't want to talk about it right now."
9. "Can you summarize?"

<u>What not to say to your husband:</u>

1. "That was stupid."
2. "Look at your friends, why can't you be like them?"
3. "When are you going to get it?"
4. "I am tired of you."
5. "Pack your things and leave this house."
6. "You are a liar."

7. "You are good for nothing."

8. "Can't you get a job?"

Simple things to Spoil your mate and Spice your Marriage
Small details that count

— Adapted from "Hylands"
(www.comienzossaludables.com/en/category/parents-corner/social-well-being)

Small details can make a big difference in a monotonous relationship. Besides brightening the other person's day, you will create an atmosphere conducive to this kind of exchange and you will also have very positive results. Following are some tips:

- The power of Post-its: leave love notes, thank-you notes or even jokes on the fridge, on the night-stand or on the bathroom mirror. You will at least make him or her smile.

- Love notes. Put a love note in his brown bag lunch, and include a treat. He will be thinking of you while enjoying his lunch.

- Prepare a special lunch for him or her to take to work. Even if you don't have time to do it daily, try to include – as a surprise – his favorite dish in his lunchbox. You will brighten his day.

- Do your partner's chores one day and make him a coffee or tea to spend some time together. Do the laundry, iron the clothes, rake the leaves in the backyard or do any other chore that is usually your partner's responsibility.

- Prepare a surprise weekend. You don't necessarily have to go anywhere. If you have kids, a weekend alone at home could be as relaxing as a mini-vacation. Make sure to arrange for childcare.

- Buy her an inexpensive token of love that will show you are thinking of her. It could be a card, a pendant or any other little something.

- Give your partner the day off. That would be a day on which your partner may decide what he or she wants to do, and you should follow along. Besides cheering him or her up, that will help you find out what he/she really enjoys doing.

There are five universal categories of languages of love according to Gary Chapman in his book The 5 Love Languages, 1995

- Word of Affirmation: compliment, encouragement.
- Quality Time: sharing, listening.
- Receiving Gifts.
- Acts of Service.
- Physical Touch.

Ephesians 5:25 (MSG)

Husbands, go all out in your love for your wives, exactly as Christ did for the church – a love marked by giving, not getting.

How are men to do that? The same way Christ loves the church: sacrificially, compassionately, gently, and lovingly. Jesus laid down his life for the church; husbands are called to give themselves unreservedly for their wives and children.

Find out what your spouse's primary love language is and communicate often in that language. It will save you a lot of apologies and "redo's" later.

Wanting to Marry

A minister was planning a wedding at the close of the Sunday morning service. After the benediction he had planned to call the couple down to be married for a brief ceremony before the congregation.

For the life of him, he couldn't think of the names of those who were to be married. "Will those wanting to get married please come to the front?" he requested.

Immediately, nine single ladies, three widows, four widowers, and six single men stepped to the front.

—Unknown

Discussion Notes

Identify the little 'foxes' in your marriage, something unnoticeable but destructive.

_____

_____

_____

What can you do to stop nagging in your marriage?

_____

_____

_____

Take Action Together

Identify practical things you can do to spoil your mate.

_____

_____

_____

What words and expressions do you plan to change or stop saying to your spouse?

_____

_____

_____

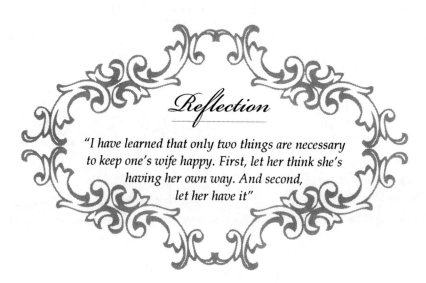

Reflection

"I have learned that only two things are necessary to keep one's wife happy. First, let her think she's having her own way. And second, let her have it"

Lyndon B. Johnson

Better or Bitter Marriage

Your Marriage Can Be Better or Bitter

There are many powerful and supernatural forces that are up against marriages. Their mission: (1) tear down the fibers of the institution of marriage; (2) shipwreck the "vessel" of the home and stop it from getting to its destination. For this reason every man and woman in the "vessel" must fight with their lives to stop these forces of aggression.

The divine institution of marriage is under constant attack today, there are now many alternatives to marriage: living together without marriage, living in polygamy, serial monogamy (with one divorce after another), and spouse swapping.

Stages of Marriage

- Stage #1 is the Ideal. That's when everyone is excited, when love is grand, and we say "our marriage is going to be different!"

    The first stage is also called the romance stage. Almost every relationship starts off here. During the romantic season of marriage, couples demonstrate intensity. They focus only on each other. Their feelings are strong, their passions are unbridled, they forgive often, and they overlook faults.

- Stage #2 is the Reality stage. In reality, the honey moon effect wears off, you see patterns as they are, and faults become more apparent. At this point you decide to adapt, attempt to correct or live together with understanding. How you manage this phase determines how you will live together.

- Stage #3 is the Ordeal. If reality is a shock and you can't cope, then you live in ordeal. The Ideal becomes an Ordeal. The ideal can turn into an ordeal. Suddenly what once attracted you to your spouse becomes the very thing that drives you crazy. Dullness may set in. Things are no longer so exciting. Nothing's really new. Disagreements turn into the cold war.

- Stage #4: New Deal. (The Rethinking stage) is when you want a new deal.

7 Commandments of Marriage

1. Thou shalt not love any other thing or person above your spouse except God. Thou shalt not let money; jobs, trinkets or even children come between you and your spouse.

2. Thou shall always find time for romance. Do little things, express your affections, buy things for each other.

3. Thou shall go on dates regularly.

    Couples who have been together for thirty, forty and even fifty years or more say that one of the things that have kept their marriage strong is going out on a "date" with their spouse on a regular basis.

4. Thou shalt not even bother trying to keep up with the Joneses.

    No two marriages are exactly the same, stop trying to make yours look like your parents.

5. Thou shalt not live in a bubble, or in a world of fantasy.

6. Thou shalt fight a clean fight.

Slamming the doors, crying and yelling are not the best ways to win arguments.

To keep your marriage brimming,
With love in the wedding cup,
Whenever you're wrong, admit it;
Whenever you're right, shut up.-Nash Ogden

7. **Honor thy mother-in-law and father-in-law.**

   Your in-laws may be incredible bores, gossipy and nosy, or so tacky and embarrassing you want to hide in your turtleneck when you're out with them. Whatever type you've inherited, welcome them with open arms whenever you see them.

Bad Habits That Could Ruin Your Marriage!

- Too busy to spend time together and on the marriage

   Many couples live as roommates, flat-mates or bedmates. They are complete strangers to one another. With heavy schedules in between, few hardly see each other, not to talk of spending time together. Over time, they drift apart and lose grip on their marriage.

- Constant interference and interruptions by the in-laws

   The presence of a third party in a marriage can make it be overcrowded. Instances where parents-in-law and uncles and aunties-in-law are heavily involved and invested in a marriage tend to do one thing: complicate it.

- Too much independence without consulting with one another

   In a healthy marriage, both parties need each another. Independent operations, doing things 'my own' way and not consulting one another before making decisions are in direct conflict to the underlying principles of marriage. Anything that emphasizes our singleness as individuals rather than togetherness as couples should be discouraged.

- Taking one another for granted ...

  Familiarity breeds contempt. This is a familiar saying that may also affect a marriage adversely. When we take our spouses for granted, we may find ourselves disrespecting each other, not valuing our mate's presence and ignoring their ideas and opinions.

- Putting money, material and people ahead of your spouse

  Money, material and other people should not to be first place in marriages. Money is a good servant, but a bad master. When given undue precedence in a marriage, money will destroy it eventually.

- Getting advice from everyone

  Too many cooks spoil the broth. Many people mean well, but their ideas are not appropriate. Some suggestions are conflicting and counterproductive while others are completely wrong and should not be followed.

Plan your strategy: don't rely on the advice of the world to bring peace into your home

The Funeral Home

The young husband was henpecked and he was going to a psychiatrist about the problem. The doctor told him, "You don't have to let your wife bully you! Go home and show her you're the boss! The young man got home, slammed the door, shook his fist in his wife's face, and growled, "From now on, you're taking orders from ME! When I get home from work, I want my supper ON the table. I want my clothes laid out. I will be going out with the boys. You will be staying home. And another thing. Do you know who's going to comb my hair, brush my teeth and tie my tie?

Yes she said: The undertaker at the Funeral home.

—Richard Benzoni, Huntington Beach, CA

Discussion Notes

What habit(s) do you think may be affecting your marriage adversely?

_____

_____

_____

Based on the discussion in this book, what stage would you say your marriage is in right now?

_____

_____

_____

Take Action Together

What actions will you take to arrest the habits ruining your relationship?

_____

_____

_____

Which of the 7 commandments of marriage do you feel you need to put into practice right now?

_____

_____

_____

Reflection

"Indifference and neglect often do much more damage than outright dislike."

10 Steps to a Better Marriage

1 out of 3 marriages end in divorce.

1 out of 50 marriages end in divorce if the couple had a church wedding.

1 out of 105 marriages end in divorce if the couple attends church regularly.

1 out of 1,155 marriages end in divorce if the couple attends church regularly and has family devotions.

Source: Francis, A.M and Mialon, H.M. 'A Diamond is Forever (2014)

Here Are 10 Steps to a Better Marriage

1. **Make your spouse' happiness a priority**
   - An unhappy marriage is like a prison cage, it drains the energy for meaningful life.
   - When unhappiness is persistent, it can shorten one's life span.
   - Happy homes have great potential for success, growth and progress. Children that grow in the midst of an unhappy marriage often have emotional challenges as they grow up.

   The Key to Happiness is to:
   - Reject selfishness, seek the other person's joy first and you will be happy too. Selfish people are often unhappy people.

- Bring your best (100%) to the marriage, not your 50%. This way you are likely to get more out of it.

- Work on yourself and your marriage, don't just fold your hands and expect the marriage to make you happy. Happy people make the marriage happy. Sad people make the marriage sad.

- Never compare your marriage and your spouse with your neighbors. You probably don't know half of the problems they face. The grass is always greener on the other side; I bet you the water bill is high!

- Make it a point of duty to meet one another's needs.

Man's Most Basic Needs	Woman's Most Basic Needs
1. Sexual Fulfillment	1. Affection
2. Companionship	2. Conversation
3. Admiration/ respect	3. Emotional security
4. Domestic Support	4. Financial Stability
5. Honesty and Openness	5. Family Commitment

To get joy, you have to give it. Follow this order.

2. **Build trust into your marriage**
    - It is a vital pillar upon which a strong marriage rests.
    - Always tell the truth. One lie renders 99% truth false.
    - Let your spouse know the details of your whereabouts.
    - Have no relationship with people of questionable character.

- Don't keep secrets. No skeleton in the closet. All passwords, bank accounts and insurance policies should be shared with each another.

Genesis 2:25 (KJV)

And they were both naked, the man and his wife, and were not ashamed.

- Let your "yes" be "yes" and your "no" be "no".
- Trust your spouse and show it. Always wear your wedding ring if you are married with one

3. **Forgive Your Spouse Often.**

Matt 6:14-15

If you forgive those who sin against you, your heavenly Father will forgive you. But if you refuse to forgive others, your Father will not forgive your sins.

- Forgiveness is the sewage that sweeps away debris out of your marriage, when it is not freely given; the foul odor suffocates your home.
- Don't hold grudges or keep malice with your spouse.
- Clean your "diaries" and settle all quarrels on a daily basis.
- Forgive as many times as they offend. If you let disagreements pile up, bitterness and hatred soon develop.

<u>What Forgiveness in Marriage Is Not</u>

- Forgiveness is not denying a wrongdoing.
- Forgiveness is not waiting for an apology or "I am sorry", though it is important.

- Forgiveness is not ceasing to feel the pain.
- Forgiveness is not forgetting.
- Forgiveness is not keeping a record and filing things away.

4. **Resolve Conflict Thoroughly And Quickly**

   <u>When you are in conflict...</u>
   - Don't get angry immediately.
   - Don't yell at each other unless the house is on fire.
   - Don't ever bring your parents' name into the fight, stay away from involving them.
   - If you must fight, fight clean.
   - Never raise your fist or voice against one another, it is a crime.

5. **Effective And Good Communication**
   - Never keep or hide your feelings.
   - Express yourself in love (tone, body language and words).
   - Be kind and courteous.
   - Listen to your wife's feelings as a husband. Don't interrupt.
   - Remember you cannot always be right.
   - Listen twice as much as you speak.

6. **Respect and Honor.**
   - Respect yourself and your spouse.
   - Never shout at your spouse or insult each another.

- Never express anger in the presence of a third party.
- Admit your mistakes, learn to say I am sorry.
- Be courteous in expressing your feelings.

7. Pray Together Regularly.

Eph 6:18

Pray at all times and on every occasion in the power of the Holy Spirit. Stay alert and be persistent in your prayers for all Christians everywhere.

- Saturate the atmosphere of your home with prayer.
- Pray for each another. Take your issues to God instead of fighting over them.

8. Spoil Your Mate

Ephesians 5:25 (MSG)

Husbands, go all out in your love for your wives, exactly as Christ did for the church – a love marked by giving, not getting.

How are men to do that? The same way Christ loves the church: sacrificially, compassionately, gently, and lovingly. Jesus laid down his life for the church; husbands are called to give themselves unreservedly for their wives and children.

It's the little things like…

1. Calling while at work.
2. Expressing appreciation.
3. Surprise gifts.
4. Give yourself completely

9. Do Not Give Up On Doing The Right Thing.

Gal 6:9. "So don't get tired of doing what is good. Don't get discouraged and give up, for we will reap a harvest of blessing at the appropriate time."

- Whether you want it or not, problems and challenges will show up.
- Stand together and fight the adversaries of your marriage.
- Don't fight one another, your spouse is not the enemy.
- Close all the exit doors of your matrimony. No retreat, no surrender...this is it for us, for life!
- Don't even play around the word "divorce" and use it as a threat or intimidation to your spouse. "Park your things out of this house" is a forbidden phrase.

10. Commit Your Marriage to The Lord Jesus

Hebrews 3:4 (KJV) For every house is builded by some man; but he that built all things is God.

A man was driving his brand new BMW along a deserted highway late one night, so he decides to see how fast the machine will go. He floors it and watches as the speedometer dial goes up to 90, 100, 110, and 120. All of a sudden, he notices flashing red lights in his rear view mirror. He pulls over and stops, and a police car stops right behind him. The cop gets out of the car, walks up to the BMW's driver's side window. The cop says, "Look, it's the end of my shift, it's Friday the 13th and I'm really tired. I'll tell you what. If you give some reason I've never heard before why you were driving so fast, I'll let you off the hook."

So the BMW driver thinks for a minute and says, "Last week my wife ran off with a cop. I thought you were bringing her back." The cop responds, "Have a nice weekend."

Discussion Notes

Which of the basic needs in marriage you feel is missing in your marriage?

_____

_____

_____

Outline which of the "steps for a better marriage" you think your marriage is urgently in need of:

_____

_____

_____

Take Action Together

Make a list of what you will do different to meet the needs of your spouse.

_____

_____

_____

How do you intend to handle conflict differently moving forward in your marriage?

_____

_____

_____

Reflection

Love is blind – marriage is
the eye-opener.

Managing Conflict and Crisis in Marriage

Is Your Marriage in Crisis?

Some studies on marriage and divorce in the United States show that about 50% people marrying for the first time end up divorced, while many who stay married are trapped in unhappy marriages.

This percentage comes, naturally, from the divorce rate. In February 2012, PolitiFact.com stated that the "overall probability of marriages now ending in divorce falls between 40% and 50%." We tend to assume that the 50% (or 60%) who stay together do so happily. There is substantial evidence to suggest the opposite — that many of the remaining couples are together but aren't happy about it.

So what goes wrong in these marriages? Frequent arguments are definitely a contributing factor. Still, these disagreements are perfectly normal. It's how one addresses and manages the conflicts that determines the success of one's marriage.

A marriage crisis typically occurs when an unusual amount of stress or unresolved conflict causes the level of anxiety to become too intense for the couple to handle. As a result, anger, resentment, dissatisfaction, frustration and hopelessness take control of the relationship. The couple typically continues the negative interactions – or disengage completely from one another, and the relationship shuts down. I call this the boiling point or marital meltdown in the marriage.

There are so many things in a marriage that can lead to conflict – issues involving children, financial burdens, meddling family members, living habits and work have been known to cause numerous disagreements. Often, the unresolved problems are brought up repeatedly, with no signs of them being ever worked out.

It is said that every marriage will be tested and tried, however our response to these tests will determine the failure or success of our union.

3 Forces that fight against our homes:

1. **The Devil**

   The main adversary behind all marital failure, the Devil, has always been desperate and determined to destroy, or at least corrupt the institution of marriage. It is his main mission.

2. **Ignorance**

   This can be described as when you just don't know or recognize the forces you are up against and how to deal with them.

   Examples: many couples don't know how to deal with their in-laws, or how to recognize a fatigued marriage (when you are just "tired" of the marriage; the solution is to take a vacation, a break together from the ordinary activities) among many others.

3. **Carelessness**

   Many couples are just negligent, period. They neglect their spouses; they won't service their marriage in order to rescue it from decay. With pressure from work, society, kids and so on, they put their marriage last.

   Please note that couples are expected to experience healthy conflict or disagreement in marriage. These are expected to be promptly managed in an amicable way and with mutual respect. When the conflicts worsen and the relationship cannot seem to return to a place of trust mutual respect and love, then the marriage is considered in crisis.

Warning Signs of a Marriage in Crisis:

1. Constant arguments and disagreements over minor issues.
2. When selfishness and an "I" spirit dominate the marriage.
3. When we take one another for granted. The respect, excitement and expectancy… has disappeared. When couples stop praying together because of the pressure of…, too busy etc.
4. When communication in marriage breaks down.
5. When the flow of love and affection decreases and "we irritate" one another. People sleep in different rooms.

Major Causes of Marital Conflict

It is said that every marriage will be tested and tried, however your response to these tests determine the failure or success of your union.

The following is a list of the top six reasons for marital conflict:

1. Financial Difficulty
2. Problems with In-Laws
3. Sexual Difficulty
4. Disagreements over Parental Duties
5. A Failure to Communicate
6. Physical, Emotional and Sexual Abuse

The Place of Money in Marriage

Money! It takes money to eat and to pay the rent, buy groceries, send kids to school, etc. Your attitude towards this valuable commodity is an important factor when the problem of money arises at home. Financial disruption and difficulty in marriage can place a strain upon the marital relationship.

Common Money Issues and Their Implications In Marriage:

    a. Inadequate supplies for running the home:

    <u>What do you do when there is not enough to spend at home?</u>

- Yell and shout at every body.
- Charge your card immediately.
- Go to God and pray.
- Accuse your wife of careless spending.
- Report your wife to your parents.

    b. When the spouse is a wasteful spender:

- Agree who manages the spending account.
- Talk together about the 'needs' in the family versus the 'wants'.
- Agree on a budget.
- Find help for a shopaholic spouse.

What is Compulsive Shopping?

Compulsive shopping is when individuals make unplanned, impromptu purchases, usually based on their moods at the given time. Compulsive shopping and spending is described as a pattern of chronic, repetitive purchasing that becomes difficult to stop and ultimately results in harmful consequences. It is defined as an impulse control disorder and has features similar to other addictive disorders without involving the use of an intoxicating drug.

What causes it?

- Inability to tolerate negative feelings.
- A need to fill an inner void.
- Excitement seeking.
- Approval seeking.
- A need to gain control.

<u>Suggestions for change:</u>

- Avoid people or places which tempt you to shop/spend.
- Cut up plastic; close charge accounts; shred credit card offers and home equity applications.
- Make lists before going to the store; buy what you need only – call support people, take a trusted friend to shop.
- Ask yourself: Do I need this or do I just want it?
- Develop better ways to manage difficult emotions.
- Develop fun things to do to fill in your time better.
- Be aware of events that trigger urges to shop like a fight or argument with your spouse.

— Adapted from Shopaholic Anonymous

    c. Using money to control and manipulate one's spouse.

This is called 'financial bullying'. It happens very often when a spouse has the upper hand financially, so at every moment of disagreement he/she uses it to their advantage to dominate the other and 'beat' him/her into submission.

<u>Signs you are living with a financially bullying spouse</u>

- Always threatens to take away the credit card, cut down on your budget etc. except....
- Demands you turn over your paycheck for their control.
- Yells, and fights with you for going over budget even slightly.
- Puts you on an allowance while he/she has free spending access.
- Giving ultimatums.
- Very secretive about income and their own spending habits.

d. Disagreeing on what the priorities are.

Priorities often differ among married couples. Failure to agree on what are the most important things to spend money on often lead to constant arguments and disagreement with fund allocations.

<u>Here are some recommended priorities a couple may consider</u>

- Buying a home together.
- Saving for the children's college education.
- Planning and saving for retirement.
- Putting extra away for difficult days.

- Taking care of your aging parents as jointly agreed upon.

How to set financial goals with your spouse

- Communicate. Don't assume your spouse will always agree.

- Compromise. You cannot always have it your own way.

- Compliance. Once the objectives have been agreed upon, try and comply. This requires self-denial and sacrifice.

- Rewards: Reward one another when financial goals are accomplished. This will serve as motivation for the next goal.

e. The problem of dealing with credit cards and debts

Debt is a major problem that troubles many marriages. The phrase 'till death do us part' has inadvertently become 'till debt do us part'. An average family in America according to statistics owe an average of $12-$15K in credit card debt. A report released by GoBankingRates, which tracks interest and banking rates nationwide, found that the average American is more than $225,000 in debt with many having less than $500 in savings.

Here are some tips on how to handle family debt without conflicts

- Be truthful to your spouse about what is owed.

- Talk together and strategize how to solve the problem. Many spouses make plans without involving their mates. This further complicates issues.

- Agree together before taking on additional financial burden.
- Avoid blaming one another for past debt. Confront it and move on.
- Contact financial experts for financial advice.
- Consolidate your debt together. It may be a smart idea to do so than to handle the debt individually.

f. Having a joint account? Easy, difficult or impossible?

Marriage advice from a personal finance columnist: Have a joint bank account with your spouse. It's the easiest, most sensible way to manage day-to-day spending and saving, and it will save you trouble if your spouse dies before you.

However there are pros and cons to a joint account and not every individual can handle it.

<u>Advantages of a Joint Account</u>

- Opportunities to discuss and interact on financial goals.
- It can bring the couple closer if well managed.
- Easy to manage bill payment and handle household needs.
- In time of illness, job loss, or death, it is easier for the other spouse to carry on with the financial responsibilities of the family.

<u>Downsides of a Joint Account</u>

- Feeling of being confined and not independent.
- May also be a source of constant argument and fighting where priorities differ.

- A lazy spouse may take advantage of it.

There are instances when a couple may not benefit from having a joint account (drug abuse issues, gambling, or addiction problems etc.). They may choose to have separate accounts with an agreed account which can be used to handle household needs. Joint accounts can work better in cases when paired with separate accounts that individual spouses can use for personal savings. On each spouse's payday, arrange an automatic transfer of an agreed-upon amount to each separate account.

g. Giving out money secretly without the knowledge of your spouse.

<u>Why does this happen?</u>

- Lack of communication.
- Forgetfulness.
- Emergencies.
- When individual have separate accounts.
- Lack of trust.

<u>Challenges:</u>

- It further widens the trust gap.
- Spouses are infuriated when there are insufficient resources, yet money is being distributed externally.
- Can create conflict, disagreement and can lead to separation.

h. Disagreement regarding giving to God's work or paying tithe.

When both parties are earning an income and only one party is paying tithes, the questions arises, "will God bless us both or individually?"

Some Thoughts about Money in Marriage

1. Place your marriage ahead of money.

2. Avoid fighting over money in all ways possible.

3. Give God first place in your priorities regarding spending.

4. Practice giving.

5. Deal with selfishness in all ramifications.

6. Attempt saving.

7. Keep out of debt.

8. Don't compare your family with others.

9. Learn to be content with what you already have.

10. Agree on budgeting.

Four guidelines:

First, there should be no secrets. Both partners must be fully aware of the family's financial status. No private income should be unknown to the other party; no deception should be allowed.

Second, there should be no master-slave attitude: "I made this money. I'll decide how it's to be spent!" The spouse working at home has as much right to the income as the other. Any income earned by either party should be shared appreciated and respected by both.

Third, there should be no cheating. Whatever plan has been established, both partners must agree to it and, if at all possible, stick to it. When that's not possible, they should talk it over and agree to make adjustments.

Fourth, the lower earning spouse should be acknowledged and appreciated in a mutually agreed upon ways particularly if the gap is in tens of thousands of dollars. Night outs, gift cards to a store of their choice, words of encouragement for their effort and submission.

Fifth, there should be no forgetting where the money comes from. Who gives a person the natural aptitudes and talents, the opportunity for education and training, his health, the strength to work, the brain to think and all the necessary equipment for earning a living? God of course. Give Him thanks and Praise often.

Spell Czechoslovakia

After a long illness, a woman died and arrived at the Gates of Heaven.

While she was waiting for Saint Peter to greet her, she peeked through the Gates. She saw a beautiful banquet table. Sitting all around were her parents and all the other people she had loved and who had died before her. They saw her and began calling greetings to her - "Hello" "How are you! "We've been waiting for you!" "Good to see you."

When Saint Peter came by, the woman said to him, "This is such a wonderful place! How do I get in?"

"You have to spell a word," Saint Peter told her.

"Which word?" the woman asked.

"Love."

The woman correctly spelled "Love" and Saint Peter welcomed her into Heaven.

About six months later, Saint Peter came to the woman and asked her to watch the Gates of Heaven for him that day. While the woman was guarding the Gates of Heaven, her husband arrived.

"I'm surprised to see you," the woman said. "How have you been?"

"Oh, I've been doing pretty well since you died," her husband told her. "I married the beautiful young nurse who took care of you while you were ill. And then I won the lottery. I sold the little house you and I lived in and bought a big mansion. And my wife and I traveled all around the world. We were on vacation and I went water skiing today. I fell, the ski hit my head, and here I am. How do I get in?"

The woman boiling with anger, though in heaven responded...

"You have to spell a word," the woman told him.

"Which word?" her husband asked.

"Czechoslovakia."

'What?' he exclaimed.

—Tamara Norden, Shorewood, WI

Discussion Notes

What are the factors that cause financial stress in a marriage?

_____

_____

_____

What are the causes of fights over money and how can we stop it?

_____

_____

_____

Take Action Together

How do you handle a situation where the spouse is using money to control and manipulate the other?

_____

_____

_____

What are the ways to handle our debt problems?

_____

_____

_____

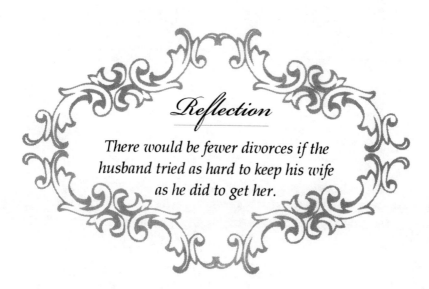

Reflection

There would be fewer divorces if the husband tried as hard to keep his wife as he did to get her.

The Issue of the In-laws

Our in-laws are part of our marriage, and think of it, we are going to become in-laws ourselves one day. The role our in-laws play varies from culture to culture. In-laws may be a blessing and a great source of inspiration and encouragement to marriages, yet they may also be the cause of friction and trouble at home.

We do not have power to control what others think or do, but our attitudes and disposition as couples go a long way to determine if in-laws will be a source of blessing or otherwise.

Read: Gen 26:34, 27:46, Ex 18:13-24, Ruth 1:1-6, 8, 14-16

What are the usual issues involving in-laws and their implications in marriages?

- The problem of the spouse leaving and cleaving to his family. Gen 2:24

- Emotional attachment of the husband to "his mom".

- Spouse always sending money secretly to their parents.

- When there is a quarrel, her parents must hear about it first.

- There is nothing she does that satisfies "his" mom.

- They are "his" parents not "my" parents.

- His parents don't like me. They are the one controlling our family. Before he makes any decision, he must first consult them.

- My parents do write me some letters, sorry I cannot show them to my husband.

Q1. What would you consider to be "interference" by your in-laws?

When they ask:

- How many times we cook meals in a week?
- How healthy is our sex life?
- Does my husband beat me?
- How much do we have in our savings?
- When do you plan to have a baby?
- When is he/she going to get a job?

Q2. How can we promote good relationships with our parents' in-law?

- Creating healthy boundaries.
- Sharing only positive things about our home and spouse.
- Open communication on our expectations.
- Take them as our parents and vice versa.
- Listen to their godly counsel.

Q3. How do I handle conflicts/quarrel between me and my spouse?

- Only call 911 if physical abuse is involved or a spouse is hurt.
- Do not make a fast phone call to your parents.
- Do not manipulate by withholding monetary privileges or bank account access.

- Pray and be patient with him.
- Find a means to resolve your differences.
- Involve your pastor/counsellor if you have an established relationship already.

What do we owe our in-laws?
- Love
- Respect and Honor
- Support (Moral, Material, Financial And Health)
- Companionship (Visit)
- Their Grand-Children (if you are able)

What Honoring My In-Laws Is Not
- Accepting all their requests and demands.
- Doing things their way at the expense of my opinions, feelings and preferences.
- Allowing them to get involved in the running of my marriage and taking over how we raise our children.
- Doing things to please them at the expense of your spouse's opinion, feeling and preferences.

Some Tips to Relating with your in-laws
- Treat them as your own parents and relate to them the same way you would do for your own parents.
- Don't take sides with your own parents.
- Make them feel welcome when they come to visit.

- Be careful of divided loyalties. Don't share your marriage secrets with them unless it is absolutely necessary and agreed upon by your spouse.

- Don't send money to your parents alone, do the same for all. Keep your transactions open to your spouse.

- If there is conflict between you and your in-laws, try and allow your spouse to help handle you them.

- Set clear and neat boundaries between your marriage and your in-laws as well as your parents.

5 Ways to Protect Your Marriage from Toxic In-Laws (Jenna D. Barry)

1. Unite as a couple.

2. Behave as an adult, interact on an equal level with your in-laws. Don't tolerate abuse and derogatory language.

3. Get out of the victim mentality. Take control of the situation.

4. Refuse to be manipulated or see yourself as a subordinate.

5. Draw boundaries and be assertive. Don't suffer in silence.

The Issue of the In-laws

Discussion Notes

What are the factors that cause conflict with in-laws in your marriage?

_____

_____

_____

What do you like about your interaction with the in-laws? What could be different?

_____

_____

_____

Take Action Together

How do we create healthy boundaries with the in-laws?

_____

_____

_____

What can we do to maintain good relationships with the in-laws?

_____

_____

_____

Reflection

"The first to Apologize is the Bravest.
The first to Forgive is the Strongest.
The first to Forget is the Happiest"

Unknown

Conflict Styles

Outwardly Aggressive

- Wolves...

Wolves are the largest members of the dog family. They can be very aggressive and ferocious. This represents the individual in a relationship who is vocal, verbal and easily picks a fight.

- Snakes/Serpents/Vipers...

Snakes are dangerous creeping reptiles whose presence is often unnoticeable. Snakes are known for their hissing, rattling, biting, and stinging. They inflict burning pain and cause inflammation where they bite. This represents the individual in a relationship who is cunning, appears to be gentle and quiet but when provoked can inflict deadly bites and toxicity. Frequently they accomplish their goals by hiding their true feelings under false concern for other people's feelings. They often act as a friendly advocate, and use this as a disguise for expressing their passion in a passive aggressive way.

- Hornets...

Hornets are types of insects that inflict deadly poison through stinging. One sting from a hornet can drive a human to insanity.

This is typical of the individual in a relationship with a poisonous tongue and words that can complicate a fight.

Inwardly Passive

- Tortoises...

Tortoises are animals shielded from predators by a shell. From old fables, they are known to be cunning and cautious. Tortoises can be very slow to react to external stimuli, and when afraid or provoked they quickly withdraw into their shells.

This speaks of an individual in a relationship who does not talk much and is not aggressive, but in the face of offense or disagreement withdraws into his/her corner. It takes great effort to pull a 'tortoise-like' person out of their shells, they just shut down.

- Chameleons...

The chameleon species is able to change their skin pigmentation. Different chameleon species are able to vary their skin pigmentation and pattern into combinations of pink, blue, red, orange, green, black, brown, light blue, yellow, turquoise, and purple

A chameleon speaks to a person whose character is slippery, they camouflaging their true self.

The chameleon in a relationship is someone that can be very difficult to understand. He/she does not reveal their true feelings about a situation and will pretend all is well when things are not.

- Weasels...

Weasels are very clever and evasive. An individual in a relationship who has weasel-like behavior can be very difficult to accept fault and usually find ways to exonerate self.

Keys for Resolving Marital Conflict

Hand grenades or land mines?

Spouses usually choose one of two ways to deal with conflict in marriage – we tend to either explode immediately or bury our feelings to be triggered at a later date. Some of us are quick to throw our anger and pain right back at our spouse when a conflict arises. Some of us avoid conflict at all costs, burying our hurt deep in the recesses of our hearts until our spouse inadvertently detonates the pain.

If you are married and you both have hand grenade personalities, explosions are probably frequent, but quick, leaving scars on your souls.

If you are married and you both have land mines personalities, explosions are rare, but huge, leaving craters in your hearts.

If you are married as a hand grenade and a land mine, watch out, you never know when the explosions will come and they inflict all kinds of damage.

Which one are you?

7 Ways to Mismanage Conflict

- Avoid, don't talk about it.

- Threaten. Tell him/her you will deal with him/her in other ways.

- Dig up the past. Go down memory lane and recall past misdeeds.

- Blame. Shift the blame to your spouse, exonerate yourself, it's all his/her fault.

- Explode. Be angry and show it, raise your fist, raise your voice and create hell in the house.

- Try to win the argument. Don't back down, don't accept defeat, how can my spouse win the fight?

- Refuse to make up. Shut down the peace process, no communication.

7 Ways to manage conflict and fight fair

- Keep a short account, don be petty.
- Think before you speak.
- Be humble and accept responsibility.
- Seek a solution quickly.
- Forgive, let it go and forget.
- Take time out if the argument becomes heated and explosive.
- Never raise your hands or shout at one another.

What to Do to Fix a Marriage in Crisis?

Note there is no quick fix or expedite process. It requires time and patience to fix your relationship. Examine the following steps to take care of crisis in your marriage the same way you would do for an automobile engine. While conflict does happen in marriage, it will take time, the help of God, ongoing support, prayer and humility on both parties to resolve crisis in marriage.

A. Check the 'warning' signs on the dashboard. This is an early indication that you have engine trouble and there is fire on the house top.

B. Are you out of lubrication (love)? Is the wine of your marriage finished?

    a. Lubrication eliminates friction

b. Buy good/quality grade of fuel and enjoy smooth running of your engine. What you pour in is what you get.

C. **Check your plugs? Are there foreign objects inside?**
   a. Outside influences: friends, relatives' opinions
   b. Distraction from jobs, children etc. that prevent spending time together?

D. **How is your fire power? Is your battery dead?**
   a. Sex life of couples.
   b. Not frequent, boring, denials, avoidance, not feeling like it etc.

E. **Radiator Overheat**
   a. Constant conflict, frequent disagreement, nagging and complaints.
   b. Breakdown in conversation, no civil and peaceful communication. Reacting instead of being pro-active.

A man was driving home from work one evening when he suddenly realized that it was his daughter's birthday and he hadn't yet bought her a gift. So, the man rushed off to the nearest toy store and asked the sales clerk, "How much is that Barbie in the window?"

The sales clerk replied in a condescending tone, "Which Barbie? We have Barbie Goes to the Gym for $19.95, Barbie Goes to the Ball for $19.95, Barbie Goes Shopping for $19.95, Barbie Goes to the Beach for $19.95, Barbie Goes Nightclubbing for $19.95, and Divorced Barbie for $265.00."

The overwhelmed man asked, "Why is the 'Divorced Barbie' $265.00 and all the others are only $19.95?" "That's obvious!" said the sales clerk. "Divorce Barbie comes with Ken's house, Ken's car, Ken's boat, and Ken's furniture."

This is the real world where relationships in families are a mess and it is in trouble. I don't have to be genius or a prophet to realize the truth of that statement. Do you not agree?

— Andrew Chan

Do you think you and your spouse are in conflict regularly? The following are signs and patterns of serious marital discord between couples:

- Regular shouting and yelling.
- Losing temper with each other over trivial matters.
- Nasty name calling.
- Extremely harsh criticisms.
- Difficulty talking about any problem calmly and reasonably.
- Throwing things at each other.
- Bringing up bad memories repeatedly.
- Being made to feel, or make another feel worthless and unwanted, or inadequate.
- Negative interpretation of your partner's views and motives.

Here are a few steps to take in resolving marital crisis:

1. Early detection is key. For many, it is already too late before they take action.
2. Identify the fundamental issues. Behind the crisis are marital principles that are being violated: money, sex, in-laws, children, infidelity etc.
3. Talk. Never let communication breakdown. Keep talking no matter what. Involve a therapist, counsellor or pastor if needs be.

4. Seek out a neutral, unbiased counselor who can intervene and meet with both spouses.

5. Be patient, pray and persevere. Problems in marriage don't just end overnight.

6. Forgive, reconcile and adapt as needed.

Discussion Notes

What do you consider the common causes of conflict in your marriage

_____

_____

_____

Based on the discussion in this book, what is your conflict style?

_____

_____

_____

Take Action Together

What can you do to minimize conflicts in your marriage?

_____

_____

_____

What ways have conflict been mismanaged in your home in the past? What will you different?

_____

_____

_____

Reflection

"Never go to bed angry with your spouse"

Abuse in Marriage

Abuse has become a major problem in many marriages today. Many spouses suffer in silence in the hands of their partners. Often the victims of abuse are so powerless, intimidated and subdued in the hands of their abusers that they often don't speak out and call for help until it is too late

Verbal Abuse

This occurs when one person uses words and body language to inappropriately criticize another person. Verbal abuse often involves 'putdowns' and name-calling intended to make the victim feel they are not worthy of love or respect, and that they do not have ability or talent.

Psychological Abuse

(Also known as mental abuse or emotional abuse) occurs when one person controls information available to another person so as to manipulate that person's sense of reality; what is acceptable and what is not acceptable.

Physical Abuse

Occurs when one person uses physical pain or threat of physical force to intimidate another person.

- Actual physical abuse may involve simple slaps or pushes, or it may involve a full on physical beating complete with punching, kicking, hair pulling, scratching, and real physical damage sufficient in some cases to require hospitalization.

- In particularly violent instances, people can die from the injuries they sustain while being physically abused. Physical abuse is occurs whether bruises or physical damage occur or not.

- Physical abuse may involve the mere threat of physical violence if the victim does not comply with the wishes of the abuser. Although there is no physical damage, it is still considered physical abuse. The threat of violence is sufficient.

Sexual Abuse

Of children or adults includes any sort of unwanted sexual contact perpetrated on a victim by an abuser.

Neglect

- Occurs when a person fails to provide for the basic needs of one or more dependents he or she is responsible for.

- Basic needs include adequate and appropriate food, shelter, clothing, hygiene, and love or care. The idea of neglect presupposes that the neglectful person is capable of being responsible, but chooses not to do so.

Economic/Financial Abuse

Economic abuse in a marriage is evident in these circumstances:

- Telling his wife to quit her job so she can stay home and take care of the kids.

- Confiscating his wife's assets and other financial resources and forbidding her from handling money or incurring expenses that he does not allow.

- Using his wife's financial assets to his advantage and depriving her of her rights to enjoy what is financially and rightfully hers.

- A variation of this economic abuse is also apparent in a relationship where the husband allows his wife to work, but regains control of her pay check and does not give her the opportunity to make any financial decisions.

Implications of Abuse in Marriage

- Bodily harm and injury. Disability.
- Sometimes death.
- Emotional scars, psychological damage.
- Effect on children who witness the abuse.
- Financial losses.
- Shame, pain, disrespect.
- Effect on the community: in-laws, church family, friends.
- Divorce.

Reflection

Marriage Is Work!
It Is Not For Lazy Folks

Infidelity in Marriage

Adultery & Extra-Marital Affairs

One of the banes of our society today is immorality as well as all manners of sexual uncleanliness. Unfortunately, there is a very high rate of marital infidelity. This has largely corrupted the institution of marriage.

> *Proverbs 5:15, 17-18 (KJV)*
>
> *Drink waters out of thine own cistern, and running waters out of thine own well. 17 Let them be only thine own, and not strangers' with thee. 18 Let thy fountain be blessed: and rejoice with the wife of thy youth.*

Here are few pointed questions to help couples identify the symptoms of infidelity in their marriage

- Have you ever cheated on your wife?

- Have you ever thought you were married to the other woman/man?

- Have you ever looked at a beautiful woman/handsome man and wished you were on the bed with them?

- Have you ever fantasied with the nude picture of an opposite sex on TV, magazine etc. leaving with you bad thoughts you would be ashamed to share with another person. (Looking on something on the internet which you quickly closed when you heard the footsteps of your wife)

- Have you ever had some close bodily contact with another member opposite sex, with your body "responding" in some funny way?

If you answer yes to one or more of these questions, you have been vulnerable. If the moment is right and the setting presents itself, you can fall into an extra-marital affair.

David and Bathsheba: A Biblical Case Scenario

Adultery and extra-marital affairs are not new to our generation. Down the history of humanity, adultery has been a problem of man. The bible documented the affairs of David in details for us to read and learn from. I suggest you read this passage and reflect on some of the lessons found therein.

2 Samuel 11:1-5 (KJV)

1 And it came to pass, after the year was expired, at the time when kings go forth to battle, that David sent Joab, and his servants with him, and all Israel; and they destroyed the children of Ammon, and besieged Rabbah. But David tarried still at Jerusalem.

2 And it came to pass in an eveningtide, that David arose from off his bed, and walked upon the roof of the king's house: and from the roof he saw a woman washing herself; and the woman was very beautiful to look upon.

3 And David sent and enquired after the woman. And one said, Is not this Bathsheba, the daughter of Eliam, the wife of Uriah the Hittite?

4 And David sent messengers, and took her; and she came in unto him, and he lay with her; for she was purified from her uncleanness: and she returned unto her house.

5 And the woman conceived, and sent and told David, and said, I am with child.

Answer yes or no:

1. David loved the Lord and had the Holy Spirit.
2. David was a careless man.
3. David was a married man starved for sex.
4. David planned to have an affair and had been stalking Bathsheba for some time.
5. David had other wives that were equally beautiful or even more beautiful than Bathsheba.
6. David forced Bathsheba.
7. Bathsheba did not love her husband.
8. Bathsheba secretly loved David. She planned it and saw it coming. She wanted to get pregnant for David.
9. All that happened was a one night stand.
10. The other wives of David were okay with what happened.
11. David and Bathsheba were ashamed by what happened and affected their families.

Why Affairs Happen

As many as 65 percent of men and 55 percent of women will have an extramarital affair by the time they are 40, according to the Journal of Psychology and Christianity. A CHRISTIANITY TODAY survey found that 23 percent of the 300 pastors who responded admitted to sexually inappropriate behavior with someone other than their wives while in the ministry.

In Dave Carder's and Duncan Jaenicke's book, Torn Asunder: Recovering from Extramarital Affairs (Moody), Carder notes that adultery and divorce rates in the evangelical population are nearly the same as the general population in the United States. Being a Christian does not lessen our chances of having an affair. Through his counseling experiences, however, Carder has found several "shared threads" woven throughout the experiences of married couples who become tangled in an affair. These patterns can serve as warning signals that married couples should be alert to.

Categories of Extra-marital Affairs

According to experts,

- There's the "Class One" affair, which is the one-night stand.

- Then, there is the "Class Two" affair, which is a love relationship that starts as a friendship and grows primarily because of a deficit in the marriage. These often have a powerful emotional connection and involve a shared task or orientation, such as a common ministry or a shared passion.

- And there is the "Class Three" affair, which involves sexual addiction.

The reasons for affairs are a combination of three different kinds of factors

1. Factors that push people into affairs:
   - Marital problems.
   - Weakness and shortcomings of individuals or relationship.
   - Excessive abstinence and sexual denial can put the spouse in jeopardy.
   - Failure to meet each other's needs.
   - Continual hurting of a spouse can make her gravitate to another man who shows affection and vice versa.

2. Factors that pull people into affairs.

These include

- Excitement, curiosity, enhanced self-image, "falling in love."
- Beware of 'Greek gifts', birthday 'gifts' given by an admirer that were not on your birthday.
- Watch out for those compliments that tend to flatter you and arouse your emotions.
- Be careful of those confidential discussions because you are the "only person they trust'.

3. Societal factors that contribute to affairs;

These include

- Excessive fascination with having 'affairs'.
- Use of sex to sell and promote products on TV, billboards etc.
- The idea that everybody does it and it is okay sometimes (Your boss, your pastor, even the president is having an affair).
- Watering down the evil of adultery and reducing it to such an innocent word as "affair". Society refuses to call a spade a spade in order to make many people feel better.

Warning Signs that your marriage is vulnerable to extra-marital affair

- Constant emotional abuse and torture.
- When bitterness and hurt are locked up inside.
- When you are too busy to spend time together and a spouse feel starved for sex.

- When you tend to compare your spouse with another consciously or unintentionally.

- When the flow of love and affection decreases and "we irritate" one another. When you feel you are tired of your spouse.

- When we fantasize about other members of the opposite sex.

What should women do to protect their husbands from falling prey to adultery?

- Pray for him.

- Make herself attractive and take care of herself.

    - Be interested in his programs and get involved.

    - Be vigilant to detect when he tends to be weak or when you perceive something is wrong.

    - Don't deny him sex.

What should men do to protect their wives from falling prey to adultery?

- Have affection for them. Listen to her complaints.

- Treat her respectfully.

- Provide her financial support.

- Don't abuse her

How to 'fire-proof' your marriage from Extra-Marital Affairs

- Be careful of unusual closeness with a member of the opposite sex who is not your spouse: colleagues, friends etc.

- Avoid meeting anyone of the opposite sex, especially individuals you are physically drawn to, in very private settings where no witnesses exist such as pub, houses, or over dinner.

- Watch your thoughts and fantasies.

- Avoid comparing your spouse with other people.

- Be honest and transparent with your spouse including details of all your relationships.

- Set boundaries for yourself: no inappropriate touching, no vulgar and unclean language, no pornography etc.

What are the implications of extra-marital affairs in a marriage?

- Opens the family to demonic attacks.

- Breakdown of the institution of marriage.

- Trust is lost.

- Respect is lost.

- Brings shame to the individual and the family.

- Affects the children adversely.

What if I have fallen into Extra-Marital Affairs?

- Let your spouse know immediately. Your spouse should be the first contact in your steps towards recovery.

- Be completely honest.

- Sever the relationship immediately, including all forms of contact: Facebook, phone, text and emails.

- Seek the help of professionals who will help you and your spouse to start afresh.

- Seek medical examination and treatment before resuming intimacy with your spouse.

- Commit to rebuilding trust with your spouse. The road may be difficult but it is not impossible.

Discussion Notes

What do you consider the common causes of infidelity in most marriages where it happens?

_____

_____

_____

In what ways do you think your marriage may be prone to extra-marital affairs?

_____

_____

_____

Take Action Together

What can you do to protect your spouse from the dangers of infidelity?

_____

_____

_____

What are the implications of extra-marital affairs on a marriage?

_____

_____

_____

Reflection

A happy marriage is the union
of two forgivers

Marriage and Divorce

One of the biggest problems that face families today is an easy, quick, and cheap divorce. We live in the age of the throw-away, or disposable marriage.

Did You Know?

- There are 100 divorces every hour in the U.S.

- A third of all divorce filings of 2011 in the U.S. contained the word "Facebook."

- The world's most expensive divorce was estimated at US$2.5 billion.

- A 99-year-old man divorced his 96-year-old wife after 77 years of marriage because he discovered an affair she had in the 1940s.

- The average divorcee takes almost 18 months to get over the split.

- Couples who live together before engagement have higher divorce rates than those who wait.

—Source: Factslide.com

Statistics	
1920	1 in 7 marriages resulted in divorce.
1940	1 in 6
1960	1 in 4
1972	1 in 3
1977	1 in 2

Now, divorces outnumber marriages! It is an epidemic! The mindset is "if it doesn't work out, just bail out!"

- The Institute for American Values study found that almost eight out of 10 couples who avoided divorce were happily married five years later. Surprising, isn't it?

- Half of all American children will witness the breakup of a parent's marriage. Of these, close to half will also see the breakup of a parent's second marriage." (Furstenberg, Peterson, Nord, and Zill, "Life Course")

- Many couples divorce, and then remarry without knowing the true cause of their marital problems in the first marriage. This is why the second marriage divorce rate is even higher than that of the first marriage!

What Is Divorce?

A divorce is a civil action to terminate a marriage. It is also called Dissolution of Marriage. It often happens when couples have irreconcilable differences that cannot be resolved.

Some Reasons Why People Get Divorced

- Money problems…bills are not paid. Fights over money.

- Challenges with Kids/ Not on the same page with their up-bringing.

- Marital infidelity: Unfaithfulness of partners.

- Not as Attractive anymore/Gained Too Much Weight, met other more attractive individuals outside.

- Abandonment (emotional, physical): Absentee spouse, loneliness.

- Abuse (Physical harm, verbal, emotional abuse etc.)

- Extended Family factor: In-laws over-bearing, rejection by extended family, third party control.

- Life goals, plans, visions and objectives differences.

- Lack of fulfillment: No joy, no peace of mind.

- Hardships of life (lack of offspring, jobs, bad health).

- Inexperience: married too early or too late.

- Other reasons
  - Wants a Bigger House
  - Wants To Move To Another City
  - Doesn't Get Along With My Family
  - Inadequate Sex Life
  - Spends Too Much Time On Phone, House Not Clean, I Don't Love Him Anymore
  - It's Not What I Expected
  - Marriage Is Harder Than I Thought
  - I really never loved him/her in the first place

Remember, it's not your love that sustains your commitment, it's your commitment that sustains your love.

The Phases of Divorce

Divorce is much more complex than it appears on the surface. Ending a marriage is not a one-time event that occurs in a courthouse; it is a process.

- Emotional Divorce.... the result of a hardened heart toward one's mate, creating an inability to give and receive love.

- Legal Divorce.... a judicial declaration that terminates the marriage contract.

- The economic divorce deals with money and property.

- The co-parental divorce deals with custody, single parent homes, and visitation.

- The community divorce involves the changes of friends and community that every divorcing person experiences.

- The psychological divorce manifests the problem of regaining individual autonomy.

Implications/Costs of Divorce

1. Loss of income...loss of savings. Debts run rampant...legal fees, alimony, child support, two separate bills etc.

2. Loss of health...suicidal attempts.

3. Loss of peace...fear of attacks, confrontations, abusive phone calls.

4. Loss of Children...loss of affection, some hatred, pain and animosity to either or both parents

5. Loss of property...Separation of what took several years to build together.

How to cope after a divorce

- It is okay to grieve. Divorce is like a death, sometimes mourning will bring the needed healing.

- Take advantage of friends and family for support.

- Seek help from professionals such as ministers, counsellors.

- Slowly but steadily get back into your routine.

- Deal with shame, pain and guilty properly.

- Don't give up on yourself or on future relationships.

Help For Single Parents (More in the next Chapter)

- Find good role models and mentors for your children to fill the gap of your ex. Raising kids is a job for two people. In the absence of the other, having a good mentor can help.

- Find job schedules that will be flexible to make it easy to attend most of the kids' functions. Try and attend as many of their special days.

- Refrain from talking ugly about your ex-spouse. It is often counter-productive and makes the kids inherit the 'bitterness' etc. you have for your spouse.

- Be civil with your ex-spouse. Fighting over matters will only make things get worse and nasty

- Plan for vacation with the kids. Do not let them feel they are disadvantaged because of the divorce.

- Ask for help when you feel overwhelmed: family, friends, church members etc. Don't lose your sanity.

Discussion Notes

What are the factors that led to your divorce?

_____
_____

How can you minimize frictions with your ex?

_____
_____
_____

Take Action

What ways can you protect your children from the negative repurcussions of your divorce?

_____
_____

What are the greatest challenges you face as a single parent?

_____
_____
_____

Reflection

"Forgiveness is the economy of the heart. Forgiveness saves the expense of anger, the cost of hatred, the waste of spirits."

Hannah More

Single Parents

It is hard enough to raise kids by two parents, therefore it is much harder when it is done by a single parent. The challenges are enormous.

Parenting Alone

Common Challenges of Raising Kids Alone:

- Stress, pressure, fatigue and sometimes feeling overwhelmed.

  Out of the 24 hours in a day, average of 16 of them are committed to work and sleep. A single parent struggles to divide the remaining 8 hours between dropping up and picking up the kids at school, working on homework and school projects, laundry, cooking, cleaning among other things. No doubt, it can be very tiring and overwhelming.

- Emotional Imbalance. It is harder in the absence of the other parent.

  A single parent often has to play the roles of both parents as different occasions demand. Male kids whose dads are not present may sometimes have difficulty relating with their fathers when they eventually showed up in their lives.

- Absence of role model.

  Male children often use their dads as their role model while girls look often to their mums to teach them certain feminine experiences. Absence of a spouse can easily present gaps for the kids as they grow into adults.

- Financial challenges.

    It is not difficult to explain that two incomes are better than one. Financial challenge results when the burden of providing for the family rests on a single spouse.

How do you handle the resentment of the kids towards the absent parent?

This is a usual phenomenon with kids growing up in the absence of the other parent. It is hard for the children not to notice the difference especially when attending functions in schools where both parents are expected to participate.

Special caution must be exercised by a single parent not to make comments to the children that may cast bad light on the absent parent otherwise the children may develop resentment towards the absent parent.

Here are few things to do when faced with such a situation:

- Prayer.
- Heart to heart conversation.
- Never speak negative about the absent parent.

What should I do if one of the children becomes difficult to deal with?

- Counselling.
- Prayer.
- Don't panic or get depressed.
- Find a mentor for the child.

Dealing With Your Ex

Dealing with an ex can be challenging especially when children are involved. Both parents need to tread carefully and relate with one another in a civil manner that will not affect the children adversely. You cannot avoid each other or stop communication. You must bury your ill feeling and resentment towards each other for the sake of the children because the kids can see these things and you may inadvertently transfer the resentment to them.

In what ways does an ex provoke you?

Unfortunately for many divorced couples, the anger, pain and bitterness resulting from the divorce linger on for a long time especially if the separation was not civil. There are things that will continually aggravate the already tensed relationships:

- Blame

    The blame game continues as each person excuses himself/herself from fault. It can be annoying when your ex points the finger that it is was your fault that the marriage broke down.

- Unfaithfulness in responsibilities.

    Another annoying issue is when the ex drops the ball and leaves the kids hanging. Failure to pick up, attend events or redeem the financial commitment agreed upon can be a continual source of provocation.

- Anger and resentment.

    It is difficult to manage anger and resentment towards an ex especially when they still display the same attitude of the past. Care must be taken not to transfer your anger to your children towards the other parent.

- Manipulations of the kids.

Never use your child to gain information or to manipulate and influence your ex. It is wrong and further complicate a fragile relationship when the children are trapped in the on-going conflict. It is painful for children when they are forced to take side against parent or testify in court as a witness against the other.

What are the ways to handle an ex in a civil manner?

- Come to a mutual agreement.

  Decide at the onset of the separation that both of you are going to work together for the sake of your children. You will not disparage each other in front of the kids, you will not engage in a brawl or verbal explosion in their presence.

  Such arrangement should be binding and if possible make them legal.

- Set the ground rules.

  Have a written and verbal rules for each other and for the children. How to treat the other parent and step parents where applicable must be spelt out and agreed upon by all parties including the kids and their new step parent.

- Let go of the past, bitterness as much as you can.

  Until you let go, true healing cannot begin.

  Forgive and forgo for your own sake. Often an ex is still holding on to grudges for several years when the other party has since moved on with their life. You rob yourself of peace and joy if you refuse to move beyond the pain and disappointment.

How do you deal with un-cooperating ex? Legally, morally and otherwise?

- Involve a lawyer.

- Don't get physical, scuffle or prolong arguments.
- Get an intermediary or a mediator involved.

"My ex is manipulating the kids against me, what do I do?"

- Involve the law.
- Mediation. Often a neutral person is needed to help resolve such conflict from escalating further.
- Talk to the kids establishing the facts. Don't feed your children with false information or half-truths. It is dangerous for them to hold on to lies into their adulthood.

How do I deal with the new spouse of my ex, especially with my kids visiting?

- Talk to your ex about what is right and wrong.
- Try and be friendly with the new spouse who is invariably step parent to your kids.
- Talk to your kids about respecting the new spouse.
- Minimize exposure where applicable.

Coping With Loneliness

One of the challenges of being a single parent is loneliness. It can be especially obvious during popular holidays and celebrations like Christmas, Easter and Thanksgiving (USA). Different people have coping mechanisms they use to handle such times.

What is loneliness?

Loneliness is the state of sadness that comes from feeling alone, isolated or cut off from others. A person can feel a lack of connection with others even when in their presence. However a person can be alone without feeling lonely.

What is the difference between being alone and loneliness?

- Loneliness refers to the emotional... the state of feeling rejected and desolate. Aloneness refers to the physical... the state of being separated from others.

- Loneliness is usually a negative experience... accompanied by feelings of hopelessness. Aloneness is can be a positive experience... a time of creativity and communion and developing self.

What are the dangers of feeling lonely?

- Frustration and anger may sometimes build when we feel lonely.

- Low self-esteem, worthlessness and excessive desire to be accepted by others.

- Suicidal thoughts and feeling of rejection.

- Desperation to hook up with someone by all means which also can lead to putting self in harm's way and temptations

What do you when you really feel down and emotionally depleted?

- Word of God.

- Good friends.

- Initiate invitations.

    - Write letters to out-of-town friends and relatives.

    - Invite people to have lunch or dinner with you.

    - Invite people to your home.

- Offer your home for meetings and social gatherings.
- Join a committee in your church that welcomes visitors or new members.
- Initiate calls to people, and ask them how they are doing.
- Service and involvement in the house of God.
- TV shows, movies, books.

How can one guard against depression?

- Right friendships, right company.
- Let go of the past, stop blaming yourself. Move on.
- Get busy, engage yourself in things you enjoy.

Discussion Notes

What do you need to do differently to make your kids have a healthy relationship with your ex?

_____

_____

_____

What are the things to avoid to keep the relationship with your ex civil?

_____

_____

_____

Take Action

It is time to move forward with your life. Make a list of what you need to do different.

_____

_____

_____

_____

_____

_____

_____

How do you handle your difficult moments (overwhelmed, loneliness, sadness)? What are the greatest temptations you face when you feel lonely? What steps will you take to overcome?

Bibliography

1. Biblical Counselling Keys by June Hunt, 1990-2008 Hope For The Heart

2. Lists To Live By, Alice Gray, Steve Stephens, John Van Diest, Multnomah Books, 1999

3. His Needs, Her Needs, Willard F Harley Jr., Revell. 2011

4. Marriage: Experience the Best, Steve Stephens, Multnomah Books, 1995

5. The Five Love Languages, Gary Chapman. Northfield Publishing, 1995

6. Prairiehome.publicradio.org/Jokeshow/gender relationship

How To Maximize The Benefits Of This Book

1. Use the copy together with your spouse and answer the questions at the end of each chapter. If you desire, coaching and counseling are available by emailing the authors at: practicaloutlines@gmail.com based on availability.

2. This book can be used for special classes and seminars related to couples and marriages in Churches. You can get your minister involved and order copies of the book in bulk at discount prices. The authors are also available on request to host special seminars in Churches and groups.

3. You can also order bulk of this book for your wedding events to bless couples who may be hurting in their marriages or to bless individuals as gifts in general.

4. The authors will be posting useful tips and resources on their website that can further strengthen relationships. Please check the website from time to time @ www.delightfulbooks.net

For More information, contact the authors at:

Jubilee Christian Church Int'l
4809 Prospectus Dr.
Durham, NC 27713

practicaloutlines@gmail.com

Website: www.delightfulbooks.net

CPSIA information can be obtained at www.ICGtesting.com
Printed in the USA
BVOW01s2138090315

390933BV00005B/19/P